ALLOSAURUS

by Arnold Ringstad

Cody Koala

An Imprint of Pop!
popbooksonline.com

| ISBN

Chapter 1

A Fearsome Hunter

Allosaurus was a large two-legged dinosaur. It was up to 35 feet (10 m) long. This is about as long as a telephone pole is tall. Half this length was its tail.

Watch a video here!

Allosaurus may have hunted in groups. The dinosaurs could have surrounded their prey.

Some scientists think Allosaurus was also a **scavenger**. It ate the bodies of dead animals.

The museum has baby Allosaurus fossils. It also has adult fossils. Scientists study these bones to learn how Allosaurus grew.

Allosaurus is the official state fossil of Utah.

Making Connections

Text-to-Self

Would you want to see an Allosaurus in real life? Why or why not?

Text-to-Text

Have you read any other books about dinosaur predators? How are they similar to or different from an Allosaurus?

Text-to-World

Allosaurus had sharp teeth and claws to help it hunt. What are some animals today that have sharp teeth or claws for hunting?

Glossary

carnivore – an animal that eats only meat.

fossil – the remains of a plant or an animal from a long time ago.

Jurassic Period – a period that lasted from about 200 million years ago to about 145 million years ago.

predator – an animal that hunts other animals.

prey – an animal that is hunted by other animals.

scavenger – an animal that eats creatures that are already dead.

Index

Online Resources

popbooksonline.com

Thanks for reading this Cody Koala book!

Scan this code* and others like it in this book, or visit the website below to make this book pop!

popbooksonline.com/allosaurus

*Scanning QR codes requires a web-enabled smart device with a QR code reader app and a camera.